Copyright © 2025 by Hannah Ward

All rights reserved.

No part of this book may be reproduced in any form or by any electronic or mechanical means, including information storage and retrieval systems, without written permission from the author, except for the use of brief quotations in a book review.

Your Haunted Home Companion, A Scary Simple Halloween How-To:

A NO-FUSS, FULL-COULOR GUIDE TO DELICIOUSLY SPOOKY TREATS, DIY DECORATIONS, AND HAUNTINGLY FUN PARTY IDEAS YOU CAN PULL OFF WITH STUFF YOU ALREADY HAVE

HANNAH WARD

How to Use This Book

"Halloween doesn't come with a rulebook—so this one is more of a spellbook. Stir, skip, or improvise as you like."

Welcome to your personal cauldron of Halloween inspiration. Whether you're planning a big party, making a spooky snack for your kid's lunchbox, or simply hoping to feel the October magic a little more this year, this book is for you.

Here's what you'll find inside:

Recipes – From cute cupcakes to creepy cocktails, there's something for every palate (and potion preference).

Decor & Crafts – Quick, low-budget DIYs that bring the haunted house vibes to your living room.

Party Plans – Fully built themes for every age group, with games, menus, and decorating tips.

31-Day Countdown – A daily calendar of mini-celebrations and easy fun for all of October.

Copy-Ready Templates – Printable-free labels, signs, and invites you can trace, tear out, or recreate by hand.

Use it like a menu, a magazine, or a monster manual. Jump around. Flip straight to what you need. Every page is here to help make your Halloween magical—even if you're doing it last minute, in sweatpants, with candy corn in one hand and a glue stick in the other.

Let's get spooky. 🤍

CONTENTS

How to Use This Book — v

1. Welcome to Halloween Magic! — 1
2. Spooky Sips & Bewitching Brews — 6
   Drinks for kids, grown-ups, and everyone in between
3. Sinisterly Sweet Treats — 13
   Desserts and candies that steal the show.
4. Creepy & Delicious Savory Bites — 20
   Savory recipes to balance all the sugar
5. DIY Decorations on a Dreadful Dime — 26
   Budget-friendly decor with big Halloween energy
6. Party Themes & Complete Plans — 32
   A party for every age group and vibe
7. Trace-Ready Templates and Ideas — 38
   No downloads. No printers. Just copy, or trace
8. Bonus Chapter 31 Days of Halloween Countdown — 48
   A Month of Magic, Mischief & Mini Moments

CHAPTER 1
WELCOME TO HALLOWEEN MAGIC!

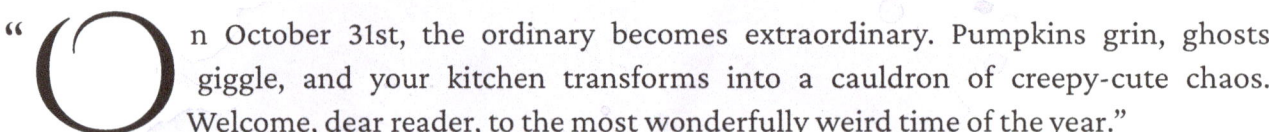

"On October 31st, the ordinary becomes extraordinary. Pumpkins grin, ghosts giggle, and your kitchen transforms into a cauldron of creepy-cute chaos. Welcome, dear reader, to the most wonderfully weird time of the year."

A Season of Spells and Sugar

Halloween isn't just a holiday—it's *a whole vibe*.

It's the crackle of leaves under your boots. The soft glow of jack-o'-lanterns lighting up porches like mischievous little beacons. It's the thrill of pretending, the joy of creating, and the universal agreement that everything is just a little more magical when it's wrapped in cobwebs.

For one glorious night, we all get to be witches, ghouls, monsters, or mad scientists—and no one bats an eye. Better yet, we get to throw parties with *eyeballs in the punch* and *fingers made of pretzels*, and everyone says, "How creative!"

This book is your ticket to turning your home into a haunted haven, your kitchen into a witch's lab, and your party into the spookiest bash on the block. Whether you're a first-time Halloween host or a seasoned sorcerer of seasonal fun, there's something here for you.

So light your black candles, grab your apron (bonus points if it's blood-spattered), and let's brew up something beautiful.

A Spooky History: Halloween in a Nutshell

Before there were plastic skeletons and glow-in-the-dark spiders, there was **Samhain** (pronounced *sow-in*), an ancient Celtic festival marking the end of the harvest and the beginning of winter—a time when the veil between the living and the dead was believed to be at its thinnest.

People lit bonfires and wore masks to ward off spirits. Centuries later, the Christian church layered its own holidays—All Saints' Day and All Hallows' Eve—on top of these older traditions. Over time, Halloween evolved from spiritual festival to playful celebration, thanks in large part to immigrants bringing their customs to North America.

Fun-sized history bites:
- **Why Jack-O'-Lanterns?** The Irish carved turnips to scare off a ghost named Stingy Jack. Americans swapped them for pumpkins (and honestly—good call).
- **Trick-or-Treating?** Rooted in medieval "souling," where poor folks went door to door offering prayers for the dead in exchange for food.
- **Witches and Black Cats?**

They became Halloween icons during a time when people believed magic was real and the lines between good and evil were blurry.

Today, Halloween is an explosion of creativity, spookiness, and sugar—and we're here to celebrate it in full color.

HOW TO USE THIS BOOK

This is your personal grimoire of Halloween ideas, so feel free to flip, skip, and dog-ear as you please.

Whether you're planning a *kid-friendly pumpkin patch party* or an *adults-only haunted cocktail soirée*, this book is organized to help you mix and match:

By Category:
- **Drinks & Brews**: Chapter 2 (because every good party needs a bubbling punch bowl)
- **Sweet Treats**: Chapter 3 (cupcakes, cookies, and creepy confections galore)
- **Savory Snacks**: Chapter 4 (mummies, monsters, and things stuffed with cheese)
- **Decorations**: Chapter 5 (DIY crafts that look like you spent hours—but didn't)
- **Party Plans**: Chapter 6 (themes, games, and how to pull it all together)
- **Last-Minute Magic**: Chapter 7 (because sometimes we blink and it's Halloween)

Planning by Party Type?
- **For Little Ghouls & Goblins** → Skip ahead to Chapters 3 and 6
- **For Adults Who Still Love Candy** → Chapters 2, 4, and 6
- **No Time, No Problem** → Chapter 7 is your life-saver
- **DIY Darlings & Crafty Creatures** → Chapter 5 is your haunted haven

Keep an eye out for Witchy Wisdom *tips,* Budget Bites, *and* Host Hacks *sprinkled throughout. They'll save your sanity (and maybe your wallet).*

HALLOWEEN PLANNING CHECKLIST

Grab a pen—this is your master plan! (Because even witches need lists.)

Pro Tip:

Make this your party-planning mantra:

"If it's cute and creepy, it's Halloween-worthy."

That's it—you're officially prepped, inspired, and ready to get spooky.

Turn the page, and let's start brewing some magic in the kitchen...

Onward to Chapter 2: *Spooky Sips & Bewitching Brews*

CHAPTER 2

SPOOKY SIPS & BEWITCHING BREWS

DRINKS FOR KIDS, GROWN-UPS, AND EVERYONE IN BETWEEN

No Halloween party is complete without a selection of spine-tingling sips. Whether you're serving up creepy-cute concoctions for kids, or conjuring bold, boozy brews for adults, these drinks are designed to dazzle. You don't need to be a bartender—or a cauldron-wielding witch—to pull these off. Just follow the potions below and prepare to impress.

So roll up your sleeves, grab your goblets, and let's get spooky with it!

Something's bubbling... Something's brewing... is it magic? Or is it just your punch bowl

MY BOOK

KID-FRIENDLY BREWS

No tricks here—just sweet, silly, and slightly slimy treats.

🖊 Witches' Brew Punch
Perfect for little goblins and ghouls who love dramatic flair.
Serves: 10–12 goblets
Prep Time: 5 minutes (+ 5 for dry ice, optional)
Ingredients:
- 1 (2-liter) bottle of lemon-lime soda (chilled)
- 1 quart pineapple juice (chilled)
- 1 pint lime sherbet
- Handful of gummy eyeballs or green grapes (frozen)
- Optional: small piece of dry ice for spooky mist (never handle with bare hands!)

Instructions:
1 In a large punch bowl, pour in the soda and pineapple juice.
2 Scoop in the lime sherbet—it'll bubble and foam like a proper potion!
3 Float in the gummy eyeballs or frozen grapes for added creepiness.
4 If using dry ice, *carefully* add a small piece right before serving, and never let kids touch or drink it directly.
5 Ladle into cups and serve with cackles.

💬 *Witchy Tip:* Serve in plastic cauldrons or clear cups with monster faces drawn on them!

Monster Milkshakes
Frankenstein-approved. Gooey, green, and guaranteed to disappear.
Serves: 4
Prep Time: 10 minutes
Ingredients:
- 4 cups vanilla ice cream
- 1/2 cup milk
- A few drops green food coloring
- Chocolate syrup (for dripping down cups)
- Candy eyeballs, sprinkles, whipped cream

Instructions:
1 Drizzle chocolate syrup down the inside of your glasses—make it messy!
2 Blend the ice cream, milk, and food coloring until smooth and slime-green.
3 Pour into prepared glasses.

4 Top with whipped cream, sprinkles, and candy eyeballs.

5 Slurp loudly for full monster effect.

💬 *Host Hack: Use crushed chocolate cookies to make "dirt" on top of the shake!*

Slime Soda Floats

Fizz, foam, and fright in every sip.

Serves: 6

Prep Time: 5 minutes

Ingredients:
- 1 liter lime soda or lemon-lime soda
- 1 pint lime sherbet or vanilla ice cream
- Green syrup or food dye (optional)
- Gummy worms (optional)

Instructions:

1 Drop one scoop of sherbet into each glass.

2 Pour soda over the sherbet slowly and watch it fizz like a bubbling cauldron.

3 Add a squiggle of syrup or dye for extra slime.
4 Drape a gummy worm over the rim for flair.

ADULT POTIONS

Brewed with a little more bite...

Black Magic Margaritas

Sinister, salty, and strangely irresistible.

Serves: 4
Prep Time: 5 minutes
Ingredients:
- 1 cup tequila
- 1/2 cup triple sec or orange liqueur
- 1/2 cup lime juice (fresh is best)
- 1/2 teaspoon activated charcoal or black food coloring
- Ice
- Black lava salt or smoked sea salt for rimming
- Lime wedges for garnish

Instructions:
1 Rim each glass with lime juice and dip into black salt.
2 In a shaker, combine tequila, triple sec, lime juice, and charcoal.
3 Shake with ice and strain into prepared glasses.
4 Garnish with a lime wedge—or a plastic bat on the rim.
💬 *Mocktail Magic: Replace tequila with sparkling limeade for a no-bo*

Poisoned Apple Cider

Warm or cold—either way, it's dangerously good.

Serves: 6
Prep Time: 10 minutes
Ingredients:
- 4 cups apple cider
- 1/2 cup cinnamon whiskey OR spiced rum
- 1/4 cup cranberry juice
- Apple slices, cinnamon sticks for garnish
- Optional: red sugar rim

Instructions:

1 Warm cider in a pot (don't boil).
2 Stir in whiskey and cranberry juice.
3 Serve in mugs or clear glasses.
4 Garnish with apple slices and a cinnamon stick.

💬 *Witchy Tip: Add a few whole cloves to your apple slices to make "poison apples" for floating garnishes.*

Vampire Sangria

A blood-red brew with bite.

Serves: 6–8

Prep Time: 10 minutes (+ chill time)

Ingredients:

- 1 bottle red wine (Cabernet or Merlot)
- 1/4 cup brandy
- 1/2 cup blood orange juice (or regular OJ + pomegranate juice)
- 1 orange, sliced
- 1 apple, chopped
- 1/2 cup pomegranate seeds
- Optional: plastic syringes for serving

Instructions:

1 In a large pitcher, combine wine, brandy, juice, and fruit.
2 Stir well and chill for 2+ hours.
3 Serve in wine glasses or pour into plastic syringes for vampire shots.

💬 *Mocktail Magic: Sub wine and brandy for grape juice and soda—kids love the deep red color!*

EXTRAS – GARNISHES & DRINK STATION SETUP

DIY Drink Garnishes

Simple details to raise the spook factor:

Candy Eyeballs

- Dab melted white chocolate into circles on wax paper
- Add a mini chocolate chip or colored candy for the iris
- Let harden and drop into drinks

Bloody Salt Rim

- Mix red food dye with coarse salt
- Dip wet glass rims into the mixture
- Great for margaritas or mocktails

CREEPY STRAWS
- Hot glue plastic spiders, bats, or tiny bones to reusable straws
- Or tie on with thin black ribbon

SPOOKY SELF-SERVE DRINK Station

Set the scene with these quick setup tips:

1. Pick a Theme:
- *Apothecary Chic*: Vintage bottles, handwritten labels
- *Witch's Corner*: Cauldron punch bowl, spellbook menu
- *Mad Lab*: Beakers, colored liquids, dry ice

2. Decorate It Up:
- Use a black tablecloth and layered gauze
- Add flickering LED candles and fake cobwebs
- Scatter mini pumpkins and skulls for effect

3. Label Every Potion:
- Use tent cards: "Bat Juice," "Goblin Grog," "Pixie Poison"
- Include a note if a drink is "Adults Only" or contains dairy

4. Stay Practical:

- Set out napkins, cups, stirrers, and a mini trash bin
- Use drink dispensers with spouts to avoid sticky messes
- Assign a goblin (or a responsible adult) to restock as needed

"With a splash of slime, a sprinkle of cinnamon, or a glug of sangria, your Halloween drink station just became a party highlight. Whether you're toasting under full moonlight or slurping from a spider cup, spooky sips bring the magic to life."

Now that your goblets are full and your potions are brewing, it's time to sweeten the deal...

CHAPTER 3
SINISTERLY SWEET TREATS
DESSERTS AND CANDIES THAT STEAL THE SHOW.

"Welcome to your haunted bakery! Here, ghosts are made of sugar, graveyards are chocolate, and monsters are adorable—not terrifying. Let your oven be your cauldron and your spatula your wand."

Halloween is the one time of year when your dessert table is *expected* to be over-the-top, sugar-loaded, and just the right amount of creepy. Whether you're baking from scratch or giving store-bought treats a monstrous makeover, this chapter will have your guests howling with delight.

Graveyard Pudding Cups

Rich, chocolatey dirt with buried treasure—and one last tombstone...

Serves: 6

Prep Time: 15 minutes

Kid Help Level: 👶👶👶 (Great for little hands!)

Ingredients:
- 2 cups chocolate pudding (store-bought or homemade)
- 6 chocolate sandwich cookies, crushed
- 6 Milano cookies (or similar oblong cookies)
- Black gel icing or edible marker
- Gummy worms, candy bones, or candy pumpkins

Instructions:

1 Spoon pudding into clear cups—this is your base.

2 Top each with a layer of crushed cookies (aka "graveyard dirt").

3 Write "RIP" or a creepy message on each Milano cookie and insert upright into the pudding.

4 Add a gummy worm peeking out or a candy bone lying flat for that "freshly buried" look.

💬 *Spooky Shortcut*: Layer these in a trifle bowl for a party-sized graveyard!

Bat Brownies

Dark, fudgy, and ready to fly off the plate.

Serves: 12

Prep Time: 10 minutes prep + 25 minutes baking

Kid Help Level: 👶👶 (Older kids can help assemble)

Ingredients:
- 1 batch of brownies (boxed mix or homemade)
- 12 Oreo cookies, halved
- Candy eyes
- A bit of frosting or melted chocolate (for "gluing")

Instructions:

1 Bake and cool your brownies. Cut into rectangles or circles.

2 Twist Oreos apart and use one side of each for the bat wings.

3 Press two Oreo halves into the sides of each brownie piece.

4 Dot frosting onto the front and attach two candy eyes.

5 Optional: Add a drizzle of red gel for vampire flair.

💬 *Batty Tip*: Serve on black paper doilies with red sprinkles for a "flying" effect.

. . .

Ghost Meringues

Sweet spirits that haunt your dessert tray with crunch and charm.

Makes: About 20 ghosts
Prep Time: 15 minutes + 1.5 hours bake time
Kid Help Level: 👶 (Best as a grown-up project or with supervision)

Ingredients:
- 4 large egg whites
- 1 cup granulated sugar
- 1/4 teaspoon cream of tartar
- 1/2 teaspoon vanilla extract
- Mini chocolate chips or edible ink for eyes

Instructions:

1 Preheat oven to 200°F (90°C). Line a baking sheet with parchment.
2 Beat egg whites and cream of tartar on medium-high speed until soft peaks form.
3 Gradually add sugar, a spoonful at a time, beating until stiff peaks form and mixture is glossy.
4 Fold in vanilla.
5 Scoop into a piping bag with a large round tip and pipe small ghost shapes onto the tray.
6 Add chocolate chip eyes while still soft.
7 Bake for 90 minutes, then turn off oven and let cool inside with the door slightly open.

💬 *Phantom Fact*: Store in an airtight container—they don't like humidity!

Candy Corn Bark

Sweet, salty, and scary-simple. No baking required!

Serves: Varies depending on how large you break the bark

Prep Time: 10 minutes + 15 minutes cooling

Kid Help Level: 🎃🎃🎃 (Perfect for preschoolers!)

Ingredients:

- 2 cups white chocolate chips or candy melts
- Candy corn
- Mini pretzels (broken into pieces)
- Mini marshmallows
- Halloween sprinkles
- Optional: orange and yellow candy melts for swirling

Instructions:

1 Melt the white chocolate in the microwave or over a double boiler.

2 Spread it into a thin, even layer on a parchment-lined baking sheet.

3 While still wet, press in the candy corn, pretzels, marshmallows, and sprinkles.

4 Melt colored candy melts and drizzle over the top for a festive swirl.

5 Chill until set, then break into jagged pieces.

💬 *Display Hack:* Serve in a glass jar labeled "Shattered Witch Wands."

CARAMEL APPLE CAULDRONS

A magical makeover for a fall classic.

Serves: 6

Prep Time: 20 minutes

Kid Help Level: 🎃🎃 (Little hands can help decorate!)

Ingredients:

- 6 small apples
- 1 bag soft caramels (about 11 oz)
- 2 tablespoons heavy cream
- White chocolate with green food coloring
- Edible glitter or Halloween sprinkles
- Pretzel sticks or black licorice "spoons"

Instructions:

1 Wash and dry apples thoroughly. Remove stems.

2 Melt the caramels and cream together until smooth.

3 Dip apples into the caramel and let cool on parchment.

4 Melt green candy melts and drizzle on top like bubbling potion.

5 Sprinkle with edible glitter or crushed green sprinkles.

6 Insert a pretzel stick as the witch's "stirring spoon."

💬 *Serving Tip*: Place on black cupcake liners with green shimmer sugar sprinkled around for cauldron effect.

Tips for Treat Tables & Displays

Make your dessert spread the center of attention.

Choose a Cohesive Color Palette
- Stick to 2–3 Halloween colors (classic orange/black, or purple/green combos)
- Use colored platters, cupcake wrappers, and napkins to tie it together

Play with Height & Texture
- Elevate platters with cake stands, overturned bowls, or crates
- Use a black gauze runner or spiderweb tablecloth to unify the look

🦴 **Add Creepy-Cute Props**
- Scatter mini bones, candy eyeballs, rubber rats, or plastic spiders
- Label treats with fun names like "Ghoul Guts" or "Witch Warts"

💬 *Host Hack*: Print or handwrite little tent cards for each dessert—makes your spread look intentional and extra fun!

Spookify Any Sweet: Fast Hacks for Store-Bought Treats

Turn boring basics into party-perfect frights.

Donut Monsters
- Add candy eyes to frosted donuts
- Drizzle with green icing "slime"
- Stuff gummy fangs into the hole

Mummy Rice Krispie Treats
- Drizzle with white chocolate "bandages"
- Add candy eyes
- Serve on black napkins

Eyeball Truffles
- Use donut holes or cake pops
- Frost with white glaze
- Add red gel veins and a candy center for the iris

Witch Hat Cupcakes
- Frost chocolate cupcakes
- Top with upside-down chocolate-dipped cones
- Add a candy "band" around the base of the cone

Sugar Cookie Jack-O'-Lanterns

- Use store-bought cookies and decorate with orange/black icing
- Let kids make their own scary faces!

💬 *Budget Cauldron*: You can glam up anything with candy eyes, food coloring, and a little imagination.

"Sugar highs are practically *mandatory on Halloween—and these sinister sweets guarantee maximum delight with minimal fright. Whether you piped ghosts, stirred caramel cauldrons, or simply stuck candy eyes on donuts, you've nailed the art of spooky treats.*"

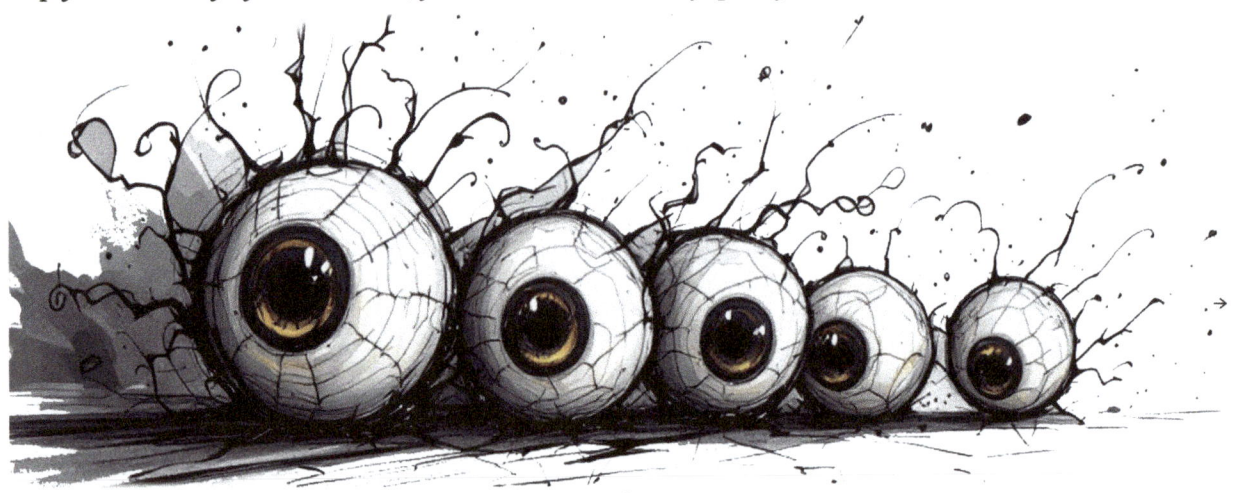

CHAPTER 4
CREEPY & DELICIOUS SAVORY BITES

SAVORY RECIPES TO BALANCE ALL THE SUGAR

"Sugar gets all the Halloween glory, but let's be honest—no party is complete without something cheesy, crispy, or wrapped in dough. These spooky-savory bites are monstrously satisfying, and they just might steal the show from the sweets!"

Whether you're hosting a party, planning a spooky family dinner, or just need a festive snack to go with your vampire movie marathon, this chapter is here to prove that savory can be just as spellbinding as sweet.

Mummy Hot Dogs

A Halloween classic that's always a hit—and super easy to make.

Serves: 8
Prep Time: 10 minutes
Cook Time: 12–15 minutes
Kid Help Level: 😊😊😊 (Let them wrap the mummies!)

Ingredients:
- 1 can refrigerated crescent roll dough
- 8 hot dogs (or veggie dogs)
- 1 slice of cheddar cheese (optional)
- Candy eyes or mustard/ketchup dots for eyes
- Cooking spray

Instructions:
1 Preheat oven to 375°F (190°C). Line a baking sheet with parchment or lightly grease.
2 Unroll the dough and cut it into thin strips (about 1/4 inch wide).
3 Optional: Wrap a strip of cheddar cheese around each hot dog before you start.
4 Wrap each dog with dough strips, leaving a small gap near the top for the "face."
5 Bake for 12–15 minutes until golden and puffed.
6 Once slightly cooled, dot on eyes using mustard, ketchup, or stick on candy eyes.

Serving Idea: Lay your mummies in a basket lined with a black-and-white striped napkin for a "wrapped and ready" look.

Jack-O'-Lantern Quesadillas

Smiling, spooky faces packed with melty goodness.

Serves: 4
Prep Time: 10 minutes
Cook Time: 5–7 minutes
Kid Help Level: 🎃🎃 (Great for cutting faces!)
Ingredients:

- 8 small flour tortillas
- 2 cups shredded cheese
- Optional fillings: beans, cooked chicken, peppers
- Butter or cooking spray
- Salsa or guacamole for dipping

Instructions:

1 Lay out 4 tortillas and fill with cheese and optional extras.
2 Using a small knife or cookie cutter, cut Jack-O'-Lantern faces into the remaining 4 tortillas.
3 Place the face tortillas on top and press down gently.
4 Heat a skillet with a little butter or spray. Cook quesadillas until golden and melty, flipping once.
5 Cut into wedges and serve with dip.

Variation: Use pumpkin-shaped cookie cutters to make mini versions for appetizers!

Stuffed Bell Pepper Monsters

Little bell pepper creatures with creepy faces.

Serves: 4
Prep Time: 20 minutes
Cook Time: 30 minutes
Kid Help Level: 🎃🎃 (Fun for decorating!)
Ingredients:

- 4 bell peppers (any color)
- 1 cup cooked rice or quinoa
- 1/2 pound cooked ground beef
- 1/2 cup salsa or tomato sauce
- 1/2 cup shredded cheese
- Black olives, mozzarella balls, cherry tomatoes (for eyes)

Instructions:

1 Preheat oven to 375°F (190°C).
2 Cut the tops off the peppers and scoop out the insides.

3 Carve spooky faces into one side of each pepper.
4 In a bowl, mix rice, meat, salsa, and cheese.
5 Spoon filling into each pepper and replace tops.
6 Bake in a covered baking dish for 30 minutes.
7 Add olive or mozzarella "eyes" with toothpicks for extra personality.
Serving Tip: Set these on a tray of lettuce "grass" for a monster garden look.

Spider Web Dip & Chips

Layered dip gets a spooky twist with a sour cream web and creepy crawlies.
Serves: Party-size
Prep Time: 15 minutes
Kid Help Level: 👶👶👶 (Squeeze bottles)
Ingredients:
- 1 can refried beans
- 1 cup guacamole
- 1 cup sour cream
- 1/2 cup salsa
- 1 cup shredded cheese
- Sliced black olives
- Optional: chopped jalapeños, or tomatoes

Instructions:
1 In a shallow dish, layer in this order:
beans, salsa, guacamole, cheese.
2 Scoop sour cream into a piping bag.
3 Snip the tip and pipe a spiral on top of the dip.
4 Use a toothpick to drag lines outward from the center to create a web.
5 Slice olives into spiders: one whole for the body, one sliced for legs.
6 Serve with tortilla chips (blue corn for an eerie look!).
Variation: Make individual dip cups with mini web designs for party-safe servings.

Eyeball Meatballs on Spaghetti

A dinner so spooky, you might just keep looking back at it...

Serves: 4
Prep Time: 15 minutes
Cook Time: 20–25 minutes
Kid Help Level: 👧👦 (Great for decorating!)
Ingredients:

- 12 meatballs (store-bought or homemade)
- 8 oz spaghetti noodles
- 2 cups marinara sauce
- 6 mozzarella balls (or sliced string cheese)
- 6 black olives (sliced into rounds)
- Fresh parsley (optional)

Instructions:

1 Cook meatballs and pasta
2 Heat sauce and mix into the pasta.
3 Plate spaghetti, top with meatballs.
4 Slice mozzarella balls into halves and place one on each meatball.
5 Add an olive slice on top for the "pupil."
6 Serve warm, and don't forget to make eerie eye contact.

Serving Tip: Present in a cauldron-style bowl labeled "Ogre Eyes & Worms."

Mini Pumpkin Pot Pies

Savory autumn magic in an adorable form.

Serves: 6
Prep Time: 25 minutes
Cook Time: 25–30 minutes
Kid Help Level: 👧👦 (Perfect for cutting faces)
Ingredients:

- 2 refrigerated pie crusts or puff pastry sheets
- 1 cup canned pumpkin (not pie filling)
- 1/2 cup shredded cheese (cheddar or gruyère)
- 1/2 cup sautéed onions, mushrooms, or diced ham
- 1 egg (for brushing)

Instructions:

1 Preheat oven to 375°F (190°C).
2 Use a round cutter or a glass to cut circles from the pie dough.

3 Mix pumpkin, cheese, and add-ins in a bowl.
4 Spoon filling onto half the circles.
5 On the other half, cut Jack-O'-Lantern faces.
6 Place a face crust on top of each filled one and crimp edges with a fork.
7 Brush with egg wash.
8 Bake for 25–30 minutes or until golden.
Variation: Add a pinch of smoked paprika for a cozy, spooky kick.

Themed Serving Tips

Make your savory spread just as enchanting as your sweets!

Use Colorful Servingware
- Black slate boards, orange ramekins, green trays
- Nestle dishes into hay bales or black gauze

Add Spooky Garnishes
- Rosemary "twigs" or chive "grass"
- Sprinkle smoked paprika, black sesame seeds, or edible glitter

Label Your Dishes with Flair
- Tent cards like:
  - "Monster Munch" (popcorn chicken)
  - "Troll Tongues" (stuffed peppers)
  - "Swamp Bites" (spinach dip)

Sketch Idea: A Halloween buffet table with layered serving heights, candlelight, cobwebs, and quirky food labels.

CHAPTER 5
DIY DECORATIONS ON A DREADFUL DIME
BUDGET-FRIENDLY DECOR WITH BIG HALLOWEEN ENERGY

"Cobwebs. Candles. Shadows on the walls. The creak of the front door...
Halloween isn't just something you celebrate—it's something you create.
And the best part? You don't need a castle's treasure to make your home hauntingly beautiful."

Welcome to your haunted home makeover. This chapter is your guide to transforming your space into a spooky showstopper using everyday materials, dollar-store finds, and a sprinkle of imagination. Whether you're hosting a monster mash, setting the scene for trick-or-treaters, or just creeping out your coffee table, these DIYs are wickedly simple and scarily stylish.

Mason Jar Lanterns

Spooky glow in a jar—easy to make, eerie to display.

Visual Note: Step-by-step sketch or photo sequence:

1 Clean jar
2 Apply tissue/mod podge
3 Add face
4 Drop in tealight
5 Final glowing display

Materials:

- Mason jars (or any clear glass jar)
- Tissue paper (orange, green, purple, white)
- Mod Podge or watered-down school glue
- Black construction paper or permanent marker
- LED tealights or fairy lights
- Ribbon, twine, or gauze (optional for top decoration)

Instructions:

1 Clean your jars and remove any labels.

2 Tear or cut tissue paper into small squares or strips.

3 Brush glue onto the outside of the jar and apply tissue, overlapping to cover it completely. Smooth gently.

4 Once dry, cut out spooky shapes from black paper: jack-o'-lantern faces, monster mouths, cat eyes, or ghostly expressions. Glue onto the front.

5 Drop in a flameless tealight and watch them glow.

6 Optional: Tie ribbon, gauze, or twine around the jar lip for added flair.

Witchy Wisdom: Use green tissue with a black zigzag mouth to make Frankenstein's monster!

Paper Bats & Hanging Ghosts

Add movement and drama with these creepy (but cute) flyers.

Materials (for bats):
- Black cardstock or construction paper
- Scissors or craft knife
- White pencil or chalk (for tracing)
- Tape, string, or sticky tack

Instructions (for bats):

1 Trace or freehand bat shapes.
2 Cut out and fold wings slightly forward to create a 3D effect.
3 Tape to walls, doors, or ceilings in a "flight path" design.

Materials (for ghosts):
- Tissue paper, cheesecloth, or white fabric scraps
- Cotton balls or balled-up paper
- String or fishing line
- Marker for faces

Instructions (for ghosts):

1 Place a cotton ball in the center of a tissue or fabric square.
2 Gather fabric around the cotton and tie below it to form a "head."
3 Draw a spooky or silly face.
4 Hang from light fixtures, ceilings, or doorways with clear thread.

🎃 *Crafty Kid Idea*: Let kids draw different ghost expressions—happy, scared, sleepy, etc.

Spooky Silhouettes (Window & Wall Designs)

From the street, your house will look haunted. From the inside, it'll feel magical.

Materials:
- Black poster board or construction paper
- Scissors or craft knife
- Tape or sticky tack
- Optional: LED lights or string lights for backlighting

Instructions:

1 Choose your silhouette design: witch on a broom, clawed hands, black cats,

lurking monsters.

2 Draw or print out your design on paper, then trace onto the poster board.

3 Cut carefully and tape to the inside of your window.

4 Place a light source behind the window (lamp, string lights) for a glowing effect.

Variation: Add red or orange tissue to "stained glass" parts like eyes or cauldrons.

Tabletop Tombstones & Potion Bottles

Mini graveyards and creepy curios you can display anywhere.

Tombstones Materials:

- Cardboard, foam board, or thick recycled boxes
- Gray paint + black and white for aging
- Marker or black paint pen
- Scissors or box cutter

Instructions (Tombstones):

1 Cut out classic tombstone shapes (rounded, pointed, cross).

2 Paint with gray base; sponge on black around edges for "moss" and white for "age spots."

3 Write names or epitaphs:

○ "R.I.P. Candy Corn Carl"

○ "Here Lies My Diet"

○ "Gone but Not Forgotten…until next Halloween"

Potion Bottles Materials:
- Empty glass bottles (any shape or size)
- Tea-stained labels (handwritten or torn paper)
- Black candle wax, twine, food coloring
- Fillings: colored water, glitter, rice, buttons, beads

Instructions (Potion Bottles):
1 Clean and dry bottles. Fill with strange ingredients.
2 Seal with cork or hot glue black wax around the top.
3 Add labels like:
  ○ "Witch's Warts"
  ○ "Eye of Newt"
  ○ "Essence of Screams"
4 Wrap with twine or fabric for a dusty apothecary look.

💬 *Budget Cauldron*: Use recycled wine or soda bottles, and mix glue with food coloring for "slime."

CREEPY CANDLES & Bloody Mirror Frames

Elegance with a side of eeriness.

Bloody Candles Materials:
- White taper candles
- Red candle or red crayon
- Matches/lighter

Instructions:
1 Light the red candle or hold a red crayon over a lit candle.
2 Carefully drip red wax down the sides of the white candle to mimic blood.
3 Let dry, then place in black candlesticks or jars.

Bloody Mirrors Materials:
- Old picture frame or mirror
- Red paint or red lipstick
- Optional: black paint, gauze, plastic spiders

Instructions:
1 Paint frame black and distress with gray/white dry brushing.
2 Use red paint to write spooky messages on the glass:
  ○ "Help Me"

- ○ "They're Behind You"
- ○ Bloody handprints or fingerprints

3 Add cobwebs or gauze around the corners.

Mood Tip: Place a single LED candle nearby to give the illusion of flickering horror.

DECORATION CHECKLISTS by Room
Stay spooky. Stay organized.

PORCH & Entryway
- Spider webs or black gauze
- Hanging ghosts or bats
- Pumpkins or jar lantern clusters
- Spooky door sign or wreath
- Flickering lights or eerie sounds (optional)

KITCHEN & Dining Room
- Black table runner or plastic spiderweb tablecloth
- Potion bottle centerpiece
- Themed napkins, plates, cups
- Edible "table scatter" (candy eyeballs, mini pumpkins)
- DIY candle clusters or lanterns

LIVING Room
- Floating bat or ghost garland
- Bloody mirror frame
- Black lace over lampshades
- Creepy silhouettes in windows
- Cozy throw pillows in Halloween colors

"CONGRATULATIONS, decorator of the dark—you've taken dollar-store supplies and turned them into a haunted wonderland. Your walls fly with bats, your mirrors bleed, your lanterns glow with ghoulish light. And you didn't even need a witch's gold. Now that the house is dressed to distress, let's throw a party they'll never forget…"

CHAPTER 6
PARTY THEMES & COMPLETE PLANS

A PARTY FOR EVERY AGE GROUP AND VIBE

"You've got the decorations. You've got the snacks. You've even got eyeballs in your spaghetti. Now it's time to bring your haunted house to life—with a party your guests will howl about for years to come."

Whether you're entertaining sugar-crazed kids, horror-loving teens, or cocktail-sipping witches and warlocks, this chapter has everything you need to plan your perfect Halloween gathering. Each party theme includes activities, food ideas, and scheduling suggestions—plus helpful checklists to keep your cauldron from boiling over.

KID-FRIENDLY BASH: *MONSTER MASH* (AGES 3–10)

Vibe: Goofy, colorful, high-energy fun

Decor Colors: Bright green, orange, purple, black

Decor Ideas: Balloons with monster faces, googly eyes on EVERYTHING, cartoonish signs like "Monster Crossing"

Theme Overview

Little monsters need room to move, play, and snack—and plenty of silliness. The *Monster Mash* theme keeps things lighthearted, structured, and easy to clean up.

Activities

Pin the Eye on the Cyclops

- Hang a poster-sized drawing of a one-eyed monster on the wall.
- Blindfold kids and give them a paper "eye" to stick on.
- Closest one wins a prize (or just a gummy worm trophy!).

DIY Monster Treat Bags

- Set out paper bags, stickers, foam shapes, markers, and googly eyes.
- Let kids decorate their own treat bags to take home.
- Bonus: This keeps them entertained while guests arrive!

Monster Freeze Dance

- Play a kid-friendly Halloween playlist
- When the music stops, everyone freezes like a mummy!
- Add themes: "Dance like a zombie!" "Freeze like a statue!"

Easy, Allergy-Aware Snacks
- **Monster Mouths**: Apple slices withccaramel and mini marshmallows or seeds for "teeth"
- **Mummy Dogs**: Hot dogs wrapped in crescent roll dough (from Chapter 4!)
- **Cheese Stick Creatures**: Draw faces on string cheese wrappers
- **Witch Hat Cookies**: Chocolate cookie base with an icecream cone, "glued" on with orange frosting
- **Juice Box Mummies**: Wrap with white tape or gauze and glue on googly eyes

Label all snacks clearly with allergen notes (nut-free, dairy-free, gluten-free, etc.)

Which Hat Cookies, Monster Mouths, and Juice Box Mummies

TEEN FRIGHT NIGHT: *HAUNTED HOUSE MOVIE NIGHT*

Vibe: Cozy, cool, and just a little creepy

Decor Colors: Black, deep red, metallics

Decor Ideas: LED candles, cobwebs, throw blankets, spooky silhouettes in the windows

Theme Overview

Teens want a chill hangout that still feels Halloweeny—minus the little kid vibe. This theme blends just enough ambiance with activities they won't roll their eyes at.

Activities

Spooky Movie Screening

Set up a TV, projector, or laptop-and-speakers setup. Choose the vibe:
- *Silly scary: Hocus Pocus, Beetlejuice, Goosebumps*
- *Mild creepy: Coraline, The Others, Scary Stories to Tell in the Dark*

Rate-the-Jump-Scare Cards

Give each guest a card and a pen. During the movie, they can rate how scary, funny, or weird each moment is.

Craft Station (Low-Mess)
- Mini pumpkin painting
- Make-your-own horror bookmarks
- Temporary tattoo table with Halloween designs

Snack Bar Setup
- "Bloody Popcorn" (white popcorn drizzled with red candy melt or strawberry syrup)
- Nacho bar with orange chips, black beans, guacamole
- Gummy worms, sour spiders, or "candy fangs"
- Vampire Punch (cranberry + orange soda) in a black cauldron
- Decorate with labels like "Zombie Bites" or "Witch Fuel"

Set up cozy spaces with bean bags, oversized pillows, and blankets. Teens love relaxed "zones."

ADULT SOIRÉE: *WITCHES & WARLOCKS* (AGES 18+)

Vibe: Darkly elegant with magical flair

Decor Colors: Black, forest green, gold, silver

Decor Ideas: Crystals, potion bottles, candlelight, moody music

Theme Overview

Dress to impress, serve magical cocktails, and lean into witchy vibes with spellbook menus and mystical corners. This party is all about ambiance, flavor, and a little friendly competition.

Activities

Potion Mixing Station

Create a self-serve cocktail/mocktail bar with fun labels:

- "Bat Blood" = Cranberry juice
- "Witch's Elixir" = Green melon liqueur or limeade
- "Phoenix Tears" = Sparkling water + edible glitter

Add fruits, herbs, and custom drink menus.

Costume Contest

Have guests vote in categories:

- Best Overall
- Most Magical
- Spookiest
- Best DIY

Tarot or Rune Corner

Set up a small mystical table with cards, candles, and a guidebook—or invite a local reader. Bonus points for velvet cloths and soft music.

Elegant, Spooky Eats

- **Charcuterie with a Dark Twist**: Add fig jam, blue cheese, blackberries
- **Deviled "Dragon Eggs"**: Use beet juice to dye the whites deep purple
- **Mini Pumpkin Pot Pies** (from Chapter 4)
- **Dark Chocolate Bark** with red drizzle and edible glitter
- **Black pasta or squid-ink risotto** for a dramatic main dish

📋 **Party Setup Checklists**
  🛠 **General Party Prep**
  - Invitations or event page sent
  - Music or playlist prepared
  - Lighting setup (candles, string lights)
  - Serving ware + napkins
  - Decor by room
  - Activities prepped
  - Food & drinks shopped and/or made
  - Costume ready
  - Favors or candy bags

🧙 **Setup Zones**
  - Entryway (first impressions!)
  - Food and drink station
  - Seating area
  - Activity/craft/game area
  - Photo or costume corner
  - Trash/recycling area
  - Emergency supplies (extra cups, napkins, tape, scissors)

Chapter Wrap-Up

> "You've planned the vibe, the food, the fun—and now the real magic begins. Whether your party is crawling with kids or full of adults in velvet cloaks and plastic fangs, these themes make sure everyone has a spook-tacular time. And if something doesn't go perfectly? Just blame it on a mischievous ghost."

Feeling a little behind on your prep? Fear not! In the next chapter, we'll wave the wand of efficiency and conjure up **Last-Minute Magic** for all you haunted hosts racing the clock.

CHAPTER 7
TRACE-READY TEMPLATES AND IDEAS
NO DOWNLOADS. NO PRINTERS. JUST COPY, OR TRACE

"Need a menu for your monster feast? A sign for your Witch's Brew bar? A spooky invite with just the right amount of charm and chill? These pages are your spellbook of party extras—no screen time required. Just grab a pen, a blank page, and a bit of Halloween spirit."

This chapter is filled with handwritten-style examples and templates you can **trace, copy, or use as inspiration**. Use tracing paper, copy by hand, or recreate your own versions based on the style shown. These are **printer-free**, old-school solutions for modern Halloween hosts.

HAND-LETTERED FOOD LABELS

Perfect for treat tables, buffets, or snack bars. Use these labels to bring humor, theme, and clarity to your spooky spread. Each one is hand-styled with a little personality.

Examples:

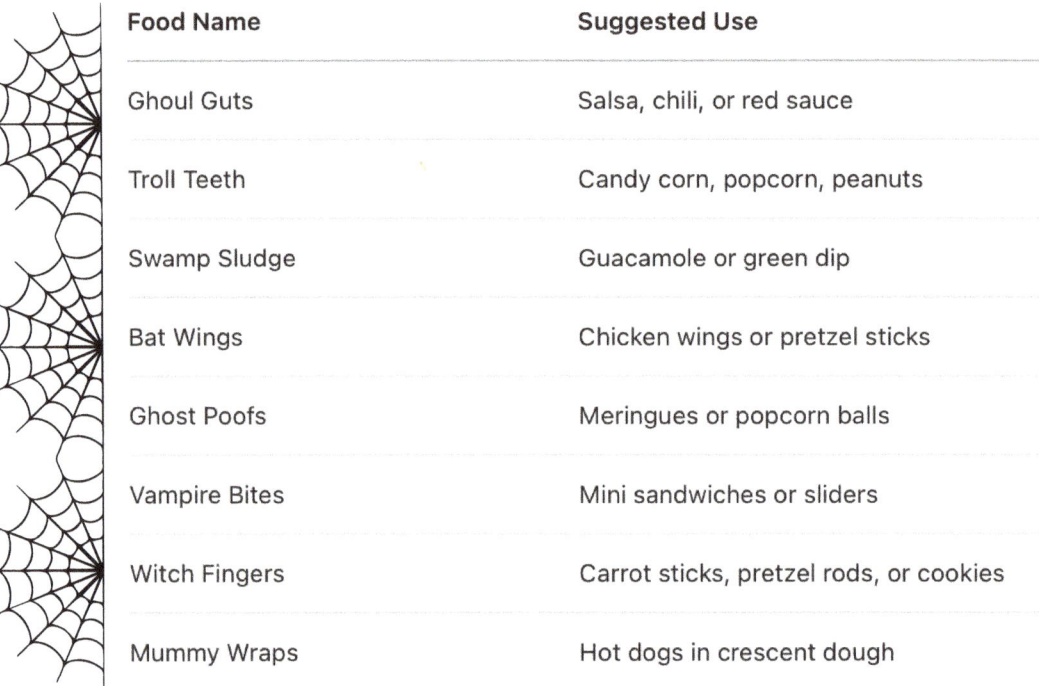

Food Name	Suggested Use
Ghoul Guts	Salsa, chili, or red sauce
Troll Teeth	Candy corn, popcorn, peanuts
Swamp Sludge	Guacamole or green dip
Bat Wings	Chicken wings or pretzel sticks
Ghost Poofs	Meringues or popcorn balls
Vampire Bites	Mini sandwiches or sliders
Witch Fingers	Carrot sticks, pretzel rods, or cookies
Mummy Wraps	Hot dogs in crescent dough

Blank Label Template Layout (to trace):

(Use your own names and copy the frame style from the printed page.)

Host Hack: **Cut pieces of card stock to match these shapes and handwrite your own food names for instant charm.**

FILL-IN-THE-BLANK INVITATIONS

Hosting a party and need invites on the fly? Use these templates for inspiration.

📎 *Design Tip: Decorate your invitations with bats, stars, candles, or broomsticks. The imperfect look adds Halloween charm.*

MONSTER MASH INVITE TEMPLATE:
Costumes encouraged. Monsters welcome!

```
You're Invited to a
🎉 MONSTER MASH! 🎉

💀 Who:    _____
🎃 What:   _____
🕸 When:   _____
🧛 Where:  _____
🧟 RSVP by: _____

Costumes encouraged. Monsters welcome!
```

🧙 **Witches & Warlocks Soirée Invite:**
🕯 Spells, spirits, and stylish attire encouraged.

```
You are hereby summoned to the
  ✦ WITCHES & WARLOCKS GATHERING ✦

Hosted by: _____
Date:      _____
Time:      _____
Location:  _____
R.S.V.P.:  _____
```

🕯 Spells, spirits, and stylish attire encouraged.

COSTUME CONTEST BALLOTS

Great for all party types. Hand these out to guests and let them vote for their favorite costumes.

✂ Tip: *Copy the design four times on a single sheet of paper, cut them into quarters, and drop into a labeled bowl or cauldron.*

```
🎃 Costume Contest Ballot 🎃

Vote for:

☐ Best Costume
☐ Spookiest Costume
☐ Most Creative
☐ Best DIY Look

My pick: _____
```

CUPCAKE TOPPERS & DRINK FLAGS

Write these onto cardstock, cut out, and glue to toothpicks or tape around straws.

🎂 **Cupcake Topper Words:**
- "Boo!"
- "Eat Me"
- "Eek!"
- "R.I.P."
- "Witch's Treat"
- "Yum or Curse?"

🍸 **Drink Flags:**
- "Witch's Brew"
- "Monster Juice"
- "Poison" (for fun, not for real!)
- "Bat Blood"
- "Slime Elixir"

✎ Use bold hand-lettering, or trace the words supplied on the next page. Decorate with mini spiders or stars!

BLACK BAT BOO!

BROOM STICK COFFIN CANDY CORN

EERIE

GHOSTS FANGS

FRIGHT

BLACK CAT BONES EEK!

CANDY CREEPY

HALLOWEEN SCARY
HAPPY MACABRE
HAUNT MONSTER
MAGIC MUMMY
MOON PARTY PUMP KIN
GRAVEYARD
HORROR OWL MID NIGHT

DIY STICKER & CUT-OUT SHAPES

THESE TRACEABLE SHAPES are reat for decorating treat bags, letters, or party corners.

📖 How to Use:
- Trace onto sticker paper or plain white paper
- Color, cut, and glue onto cards, bags, or boxes
- Use as table scatter or in craft activities

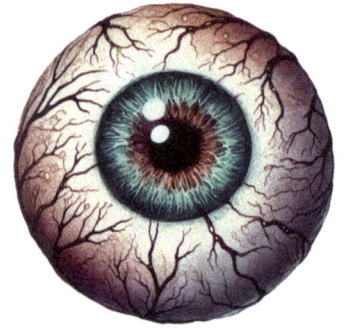

🤍 KID TIP: Let children color in blank versions and make their own spooky stickers!

Tips for Tracing Without Special Supplies:

- Use a bright window: Tape the template page and your tracing paper to a sunny window to see outlines clearly.
- Use tracing paper, wax paper, or even parchment paper.
- Don't worry about perfection—imperfect lines = handmade charm!

Tools You Might Use:

- Markers or felt-tip pens
- Colored pencils
- Scissors
- Glue stick
- Toothpicks or straws (for toppers/flags)
- Yarn or ribbon (for banners)

"Your party is now fully labeled, signed, and sealed with spooky love. From banner letters to snack tags, you've created hand-crafted Halloween magic—without a single digital download. Your guests will think you spent hours on the details. We'll keep your secret."

🎃 Now go forth, dear party wizard, and may your Halloween be wickedly fun, deliciously eerie, and deeply memorable.

CHAPTER 8
BONUS CHAPTER 31 DAYS OF HALLOWEEN COUNTDOWN
A MONTH OF MAGIC, MISCHIEF & MINI MOMENTS

"October is for the dreamers, the dress-up lovers, the candy samplers, the light-switch prankers. It's 31 days of creepy charm, cobwebby corners, and moments so small they feel like magic."

Welcome to your Halloween warm-up. This countdown gives you **one tiny treat, tip, or tradition per day**—no elaborate planning, no special supplies, no stress.

with your coven of grown-up ghouls, these ideas are bite-sized and packed with spooky joy.Just flip, read, do, and smile. Whether you're doing this solo, with your kids, or
Use this section daily, or whenever you need a dose of haunted happiness.

31 Days of Halloween Countdown

SUN	MON	TUE	WED	THU	FRI	SAT
	1 🎃 Decorate ONE room — just start.	2 🍎 Monster Mouths (apple + marshmallows)	3 👀 Googly eyes in the fridge!	4 🦇 Cut 5 paper bats + fly them up a wall	5 🎵 Halloween music while cooking	6 🧡 Eat something orange today
7 🍌 Draw jack-o'-lantern faces on bananas	8 🕯️ Dinner by candlelight = haunted mansion vibes	9 👻 Make a tissue ghost + name it	10 🎬 Watch a Halloween movie (*Casper*, *Hocus Pocus*)	11 👢 Wear something black, striped, or spooky	12 🕷️ Hide a plastic spider in someone's shoe	13 🏚️ Draw a haunted house
14 👁️ Stick paper eyeballs on your windows	15 🍕 Rename your food: "Ghoul Guts" = salsa!	16 📖 Write a 3-sentence ghost story	17 🧙 Try on a costume—even if it's silly	18 💧 Write "BOO" on your mirror	19 🔦 Flashlight snack time in the dark	20 🦇 Make + wear bat wings
21 🧙 Dinner talk: witches + vampires only	22 📦 Build a haunted house from a box	23 👤 Whisper a spooky (or silly) tale	24 🥤 Make a smoothie + call it *Monster Sludge*	25 🧸 Give a toy its own Halloween costume	26 ✍️ Read or write a Halloween poem	27 👻 Tape paper ghosts to your ceiling
28 🎃 Play a harmless Halloween prank	29 🍬 Set out a candy bowl for "practice"	30 🔍 Make a 5-item Halloween scavenger hunt	31 🎉 Happy Halloween! Take a photo + treat yourself!			

October 1 – Set the Scene

Pick *one* room to start decorating. Add a pumpkin, a candle, or a paper bat. One thing. That's all it takes to open the portal to Halloween season.

October 2 – Monster Mouth Snack

Make apple slice "monster mouths" by sandwiching sunflower butter (or cream cheese) between two slices. Add mini marshmallow "teeth." Bonus: make them scream.

October 3 – The Fridge Is Watching You

Stick googly eyes on everything in your fridge. Milk. Ketchup. Leftovers. Then open the door dramatically and gasp like you've just seen a ghost.

October 4 – Bat Attack!

Cut out five paper bats and tape them flying up a door or wall. Don't worry about perfection. Crooked wings are more authentic.

October 5 – Haunted House Soundtrack

Play a Halloween playlist while brushing your teeth or making dinner. Dance like a zombie. Stir the pot like a witch.

October 6 – Snack Something Orange

Today's mission: Eat something orange. It could be cheddar cheese, a clementine, or candy corn. Bonus: Eat it while watching a black-and-white horror film.

October 7 – Banana Boos

Draw jack-o'-lantern faces on bananas with a marker. Pack them in lunches or line them up on the counter for your family of ghost-fruit.

October 8 – Haunted Dinner Hour

Eat dinner in candlelight. Turn off the overheads, light a candle or two, and pretend you're in a haunted mansion. Speak only in spooky voices.

October 9 – Adopt a Tissue Ghost

Make a ghost out of a tissue and cotton ball. Draw a face. Give it a name. Carry it in your pocket. Yes, even to work.

October 10 – Movie Night Lite

Watch a non-scary Halloween movie tonight. Good picks: *Casper*, *Coraline*, *Hocus Pocus*, or *Wallace & Gromit: The Curse of the Were-Rabbit*.

October 11 – Dress the Part

Wear something Halloweeny today—black and orange, a striped sock, spider earrings, a hoodie with bat ears. Bonus points if it makes someone smile.

October 12 – Hide the Spider

Take a small plastic spider (or draw one on paper) and hide it somewhere unexpected—shoe, fridge, pillow. Wait for the scream. Or giggle.

October 13 – Doodle a Haunted House

Draw the weirdest, wildest haunted house you can imagine. Is it in a tree? A castle? Made of cake? No rules. Just draw.

October 14 – Eyes on Everything

Cut out paper eyeballs and stick them on windows, lamps, or picture frames. Suddenly, your whole house is watching…

October 15 – Rename Your Snacks

Whatever you eat today, rename it. Chips? *Dragon Scales*. Grapes? *Witch Warts*. Pizza? *Flatbread from the Underworld.* Say it aloud with a flourish.

October 16 – Write a Ghost Story (In 3 Sentences)

Short. Sweet. Spine-chilling. Share it with a friend, write it on a napkin, or whisper it into the dark.

October 17 – Costume Preview

Try on a costume—or improvise one from what you already have. A towel can be a cape. A belt? A ghostbuster gadget. Have a laugh.

October 18 – Mirror Message

Write "BOO!" on your bathroom mirror with lipstick, dry-erase marker, or a sticky note. Freak yourself out. Then grin at your reflection.

OCTOBER 19 – Flashlight Feast

Eat a snack or dinner in the dark... with flashlights under your chin. Tell a spooky story while chewing. Atmospheric and delicious.

October 20 – Become a Bat

Make wings from paper or cardboard and wear them around the house. Bonus: Crawl across the floor and whisper, "I'm nocturnal..."

October 21 – Witches at the Table

Tonight, everyone at the dinner table must talk like a witch, warlock, ghost, or vampire. No breaks. Cackles required.

October 22 – Build a Haunted Mini House

Use a shoebox or cardboard scraps to build a spooky diorama. Add stick ghosts, paper gravestones, and a tiny pumpkin made of a wad of gum.

October 23 – Whisper a Tale

Tell a ghost story in a whisper. Even if it's silly. Especially if it's silly.

October 24 – Make a Monster Smoothie

Blend bananas, frozen berries, and yogurt. Add a squirt of food coloring if you like. Call it *Monster Sludge* and drink it with pride.

October 25 – Costume a Toy

Pick a stuffed animal or doll and make it a costume. Paper crown, bat wings, googly eyes. Introduce it to the family.

October 26 – Read a Poem (Or Write One!)

Halloween poems are the best kind of nonsense. Read one aloud, or make your own: "Roses are red, violets are blue, my socks are haunted, and so is my shoe."

October 27 – Ceiling Ghosts

Cut out paper ghosts and tape them to your ceiling. When you lie in bed, they'll float above you. Sleep well...

October 28 – Trick Time

Pull a harmless prank today. Hide behind a door. Scream softly. Switch someone's phone wallpaper to a mummy. Giggle like a ghoul.

October 29 – Candy Bowl Practice

Fill a bowl with candy. Eat one. Practice saying "Happy Halloween!" in your best Dracula voice. Repeat. For science.

October 30 – Scavenger Hunt!

Make a 5-item Halloween scavenger list: something orange, something round, something spooky, something black, and a hidden treat. Go find them!

October 31 – Celebrate!

It's Halloween! Snap a spooky photo. Say your best spell. Eat your favorite treat. Take a deep breath and smile—you made a whole month of magic.

"Halloween isn't just one night—it's a whole season, one cobweb, costume,

and cackle at a time.

Thanks for counting it down with us.

And remember: every October holds 31 doors. You just opened them all."

www.ingramcontent.com/pod-product-compliance
Lightning Source LLC
LaVergne TN
LVHW070218080526
838202LV00067B/6844